LIVING WARRIORS

Folkestone, March 2019

A Living Words project

Living Warriors
Folkestone, March 2019

Publisher: Independent Publishing Network
Publication date: May 2019
ISBN: 978-1-78972-295-6
Author: Living Words
Email: info@livingwords.org.uk
Address: GF01, The Glassworks, Mill Bay, Folkestone CT20 1JR
Website: www.livingwords.org.uk
Please direct all enquiries to the author

Images on page 3 & 60 by Ethan Sheppard

Introduction

In March 2019, three groups of strangers started meeting at Folkestone library in their own unique, hand made, 'you can write on the walls' space. What unfolded over the following month could not have been predicted.

Brought together to share stories of the moments in which we chose not to end our lives, we were all very different on the outside. We spent one-to-one time with Living Words writers, in our secret pods, emerging (as Madlin rang the cow bell) to share our experience and words with each other. We heard and felt the similarities between us - in the language we used, the love we felt, the fights we fought, the way we were still standing, and the recognition of how hard living can sometimes be. Our words became personal books, edited with the writers in the Living Words method, to clearly be our voices.

Whilst this short project ended. Our individual books and this anthology of some of our pieces, is our legacy. Though this group ends, we see each other in our hearts, our minds and on the streets of Folkestone.

Peace Out

The Living Warriors

Individuals...together...as survivors...in Folkestone

Contents

I have endeavoured to live a life of love and kindness
towards others.

I think it's only love and kindness
which fills the inner gap.
People try to fill the inner gap with other things,
but those things don't work long-term.

Yeah, that's my philosophy.

Andrew Welcome

MOMENT 1

It wasn't a moment, just a gradual work up. And after the therapy finished I was on three different meds, couldn't find the right one. It took me two years to find Mirtazapine and that seemed to help me sleep because I wasn't sleeping.

About three months on that and it really helped me. And anyone on drugs will tell you – when you start to feel better, you think you are better and start to take yourself off. I was "I feel better now I'm going to take myself off" and that's what I did.

I was walking down the beach and walking down the pier and I would walk as close to the edge as possible – 'If I trip now it will be fine, it wont be my fault, I just tripped'. And one of those days I walked down to the end of the pier and stood on the ledge and I was just there swaying backwards and forwards 'If the wind catches me, it's not my fault, I'm just up here'. Cos in my head I was 'It can't be my fault'. But then you know it is. You are putting yourself in that situation.
And when I was up on that ledge-part of the pier I felt ready, but at the same time you look out and see Dover and everything. And I saw...

I don't know. Don't know how to describe it, you aren't thinking – you are in kind of a blind spot.
But all these little things in your head moving around

And my mum just kept coming back in my head all the time
And that time I still sort of believed in God, so 'If you do it now, am I going to get into paradise?'
All that internal panic
'Will I ever see my family again?'
And it just freaked me out so much, I kind of blacked out.
And then this woman was there and she asked me if I was ok and I was like, "Yeah, fine".

So I just got down and walked home and cried my eyes out.

Ethan Sheppard

Wow, straight away – Burden

Always comes in my head when I think of suicide
always that big word 'burden'.

Always straight in my head – 'burden'
Not just a burden to people, but a burden to life in
general
Like, if you can get out of the world you're not going to
be painful for anyone else
Cos you always know that you are hurting people, and
it's the last thing you're gonna do – hurt people.

Always such a taboo subject as well
you know as soon as you see the word 'suicide'
people start panicking or run for the hills or think 'don't
mention the word dying or anything'
You just think 'No'

TJ Frost

Not everybody's found dead in bed like Marilyn Monroe

I think the ultimate feeling was, I felt a coward.
Because of the method I'd chosen, which was pills, I
started to think about the impact if I failed.

Suicide is almost like a leap of faith.
Is where I'm going, going to correlate with what I'm
leaving?

I haven't got the guts in taking my own life. If I didn't do
it properly, could I leave myself in a more debilitated
state?

Which would then lead to me becoming more of a
burden than I already was,
or felt that I was at that point,
or more useless to society?

Was it going to devalue me any more than what I
already felt devalued?

You know, I'd like to think it was nice, flowery gardens
with my grandmother sitting there, but equally, it might
not be.
It might be somewhere quite dire.
or I might wake up somewhere significantly different,
somewhere I've got to do this all over again 10 times.

I would like to say I was thinking about my family and friends and all that I would leave behind.
I'd already pre-recorded messages, and I didn't see myself as great value to them.

My reasons were purely selfish.
They were mine alone.
I remember thinking about this 1920s movie star, Villaise, in a book called Hollywood Babylon.
She ended her life. She took pills and washed them down with a large amount of alcohol, and obviously she intended to be found laid out on the bed, and to be surrounded by flower garlands.

She was actually found with her head down the toilet.
It was not as she intended, and it was clear that she died in some agony.

That didn't end well.
It ended, but it didn't end well.
She didn't just lay down and go to sleep.

Not everybody's found dead in bed like Marilyn Monroe.

Elizabeth

It's bonkers isn't it?

I drove my car into a wall.
Slammed my car into a wall.
Well, that's not really gonna work is it?

I wouldn't say I got less mad.
Categorically, what stopped me was my sense of
humour.
The ability to laugh at what you're planning and think ,
"This is ridiculous".

I thought, "I'm gonna hang myself from the loft ladder."
But then,
"Oh god what about the dog? The dog's gonna have to
eat me.
And what if the postman finds me? That's not going to
be very nice for the postman."
"How could I make it so he won't smell me?"

And I thought, "Well I could clip those little Magic Trees
all over me. Maybe that would stop the smell?"
That's what I mean about the humour.

Sally Ann Cranage

Decades and decades ago
Another world – it's so weird
When talking about it – it's playing out like a film
An old cocktail cabinet
Swigging out of the bottles
I can see myself doing it
Panicking in the kitchen 'Put that back'
One of them just got up to go to the toilet

That was it

I thought 'Quick, before they get home'
And then I just sat there
And listened to music until they pulled up
And I turned it off
Thought 'Shit, they're home'
And then the curtain comes down
Funny

TJ Frost

Lining everything up

I compare it to writing a letter in the olden days.
You used to be slow doing it.
You would have to have the paper, the time and the inclination to write and a stamp.
In a sense, contemplating suicide is like that: Everything has to line up.

There are all these moments where if someone can just break that and not let things line up then that can just be so effective.

For me, it has been my brother stepping in.
I know that since my last episode of depression, I have talked about it so much more because that was one of the ways for me to make sense of it.

I know I have had discussions with friends about suicide in such a light-hearted way, but that's still been at really important moments - and this is sometimes for them rather than for me.

Lubna Gem Arielle

Look Up

I will never be the same again
But he wouldn't want me to take my life
Not be smiling
He is also keeping me going
Because he'd want me to keep going

That's why I've got this tattoo for him:
'Don't look down mummy'
Don't look down at his grave – look up and around,
Look to other things that can cause joy
And look to other things that can keep me going

India Gibson

Resilience and gaining confidence

I
What stopped me?
Guilt. Yeah, guilt
Determination to strike back
To not give up
To regain hope
I never lost full hope

II
I'm pretty resilient
With my challenges
My life experiences
I haven't exactly been around ages either
Only 33 years!

III

Major progression:
Sad but at the same time glad
I've come this far with my progress -
on my mental health
on my learning differences

Sam

I remember when my grandma died, whose name I've
got, she said to my mum,
      'It's not the dying you got to worry about,
      It's the living.'

Because the dead have gone,
hopefully they're settle wherever they go.
But the living have to pick up the pieces after someone
has gone.

I think it would be selfish to kill myself,
and leave destruction behind.

Kat

October 21, 2015

Back-to-the-future day. You know, from the film? The
actual date they go to - that date came up. I remember
seeing that film as a child. I was thinking, "Oh my god,
this is my future".
At that point I had left my parents. I was renting a flat in
East Finchley. It was a nice enough flat. Most of my stuff
was in storage. I was still on meds. I was having
nightmares about the situation in my old flat. I
remember thinking, "My God, it's back to the the future
day and here I am".

During this time, I was seeing my psychiatrist.
He had once turned to me and said - (bearing in mind
he'd known my for 19 years from the previous episode)
He said, "Lubna, the thing about you -" (and I thought
he was going to say something nice and healing) - "The
thing about you, is at this stage of your life, you should
be married and have a family and also be a partner in a
law firm." Because he knew I used to be a lawyer. I was
livid about him saying that.

Back-to-the-future-day
That was a judgement I was having about myself.

He said I should be in a stable career. All this framework
of life that does not apply to me - that I'm just not
interested in. So this particular day was such a weird
day.

I could feel myself sinking and sinking and sinking but -
then, I heard the sound of fireworks. It wasn't anywhere
near firework day. I went outside and I saw fireworks
just at the end of the street which was just bizarre. The
neighbour came out and she stood there with me.
It comes back to that thing of somehow the pattern
being broken - of there being this moment - a moment
where I'm so close and then - something - in this case

not my brother - but something *so* out of the ordinary.
If I now think about it, it's something that breaks the
pattern. Whether that's the vodka and the pills not
being the right balance, or my brother twice or the
fireworks.
The next day, when I saw the neighbour, because it had
been so bewildering I had said, "We were there
yesterday weren't we? We did see those fireworks?" It
was just so bizarre.
It was uplifting for me. There's something about that
story - there's a lot of hope in it.

Lubna Gem Arielle

I &

POWER IN ME

IAM ALIVE

WOOP! WOOP!

WON X — X —

| WON |

A UP INTHE SKY!!!

His little light of mine

Everything I do is for you. You keep me strong!

LOOK UP

glad to be

GRATITUDE xxxx

I have grown! Blossoming

GETTING BIGGER + STRONGER!
X

Feeling loved

WOW! CONSISTENCY

10 xx

Blue skies

SUC cess

IT'S GOING TO BE OK!! Be yourself

like a strongly rooted tree on a strong breeze and after, still rooted and a freshness in the air

I feel a s
I have imp
and ambitio
about how my c
Shape who I am

Strong but
strength

climbing
mountain

24

Feelings

15-16 years
A very long process.
When I got arrested, I definitely wanted to kill myself.
Well, I don't know if I wanted to kill myself?
Just wanted everything to stop -
Wanted my head to stop.
Absolutely immobilised with myself.
Absolutely frightened -
Frightened of all those feelings.

But then,
being so frightened of those feelings,
I had been frightened to be happy as well.
I was so frightened of those mental feelings,
I didn't let happiness in as well.

I had to do the pain.
Had to do the grief -
Particularly the grief.
Had to process all that stuff
To then eventually be happy.
I didn't do crying.
"If I'm not going to be sad,
I'm not going to be happy either."
Had to process grief to find happiness.

I was in the empty void.
That's why I was so empty.

I didn't have any feelings - and -
If I did have feelings,
I couldn't identify them -
because - I'd never done that.
That had been fixed from such a young age,
From 12-13 until 38-39.
It's a long time not to have feelings.
Apart from humour!

Sally Ann Cranage

Do you remember Knight Rider?

I couldn't stand him and his hair – superficial, ugly
I thought 'Oh My God'
All the girls fancied him – the bloody posters. Sod off!
I was in love with the car.

Why?
Because that car protected him
He would have been fuck all without that car
Oh you swan around like one, 'No. Mate – I'm in love
with your car'
And it wasn't like it was some posh thing
It was because it spoke and it looked after him
That was my connection.

Just goes to show you
It was a bit of metal
but it looked out for him.

It doesn't matter what shape or form.

TJ Frost

Space of time

I didn't fully expect to defeat them twice,
Those feelings and experiences,
I'm proud of that.

It's an achievement -
To have these adversities
To come out towards the other end

There's loads -
Too much to say
In this short space of time

Sam

BRAVE

1

I don't feel brave
I've got people telling me I'm brave every day
All I'm doing is trying to get through the next day
Or hour, or week
For me it is just persevering

So when people tell you "You are brave"
I'm strong because I have to be
Not because I want to be
Otherwise I wouldn't be here

India Gibson

I can't remember the moment, the day, when I realised
I was depressed.
Cos it's not like one day you just realise 'Oh I'm
depressed'. You gradually go into it and hopefully you
gradually come out of it.
And I kind of walked into this space
feeling numb all the time.

I didn't understand why my friends were doing things
and I couldn't feel the same way.

In my family I wasn't enjoy things,
I just wanted to be alone in my room and sleeping all
the time.
I was feeling really confused, but at the same time:
my parents were going through a separation.
my brother was going fucking mental, with police
coming up every weekend - he was bashing on the
doors, trying to break in, smashing windows. He tried to
strangle me once, that was fun.
Fights with my dad.
That kind of thing.
And on top of all that I was 'I'm gay, I'm a Jehovah's
Witness and this is all awful'.

So, yeah – I was raised religious as well, so I had this
whole mentality in my head.
All these things – swimming
around my head at the same time.

So I retreated into myself and that's when I started self harming.

And it wasn't until a month or so in, I remember actually we were in PSHE in school and the teacher was talking about mental health and self harm
and I was "What's that?"
and she was "It's when people hurt themselves differently, for whatever reason"
and I was 'Oh that's literally what I've been doing'.

And it wasn't until I guess a month after that, that I really started questioning *why* I was self harming.
And I kind of realised it was because – when you are internally having all this struggle, all this anxiety and depression – there's nowhere for it to go.

So when you self harm in whatever means
– I would cut and burn myself a little bit. Used to punch myself red raw –
it was that way to have that physical thing on you
that you can watch heal – a way of expressing it

Getting it out – watching it heal – for me it was – watching it
Why is that healing but I am not, inside?
And it really confused me for a while.
I think I only self harmed for about a year, year and a half. I think. It was bad.

Ethan Sheppard

I think sometimes suicide is glamourised in films. And songs.

Songs that have the subject of suicide, they almost make it sound romantic.
That someone will find you.
That eventually someone's going to save you.

There's a poignant video by Britney Spears, called *Always*.
She's in the bath, trying to kill herself, and a man runs in and finds her.

But it isn't a happy ending.

Kat

I'm Not Bloody Selfish!

People make you feel guilty and that horrible word –
suicide equals selfish
That is one of the big painful things –
"How could you be so selfish?"
"Why would you do that to your kids?"
"Why would you do that to your grandkids?"
And it's just that same thing again
 "Can't you see it's like I am trying to protect you? I am
trying to protect that beautifulness"

It's like I'm ugly
Just a blob
A blob of nothing and everything
So if I come away from that
It's not going to make that ugly.

It's like a disease.
Like I'm a horrible disease.
Like I'm going to taint people around with that ugliness.
It's like – "Just get away"

I am thinking of Others all the bloody time
Always about the others –
To me, that is where the misunderstanding is
I am not bloody selfish

TJ Frost

2.

On bad days when I cut myself I would use my own blood, and start drawing and painting and things. A bit gross.
At the time it felt great – like a real expression of my internal struggle.

Cos for me, personally growing up a witness – you don't share blood, it's very personal. Part of you and your 'soul', your make up.

So using *that* as an art-form to make a picture was: "This is mine. This is literally my 'soul', right now." And it felt like shit.

Ethan Sheppard

You Are Not a Burden!

I don't like to worry people
Since losing Toby, I didn't want to add extra stress to
everyone
I knew that I'd got through
And to me, that was enough

Really stupid – not stupid – but I know I shouldn't feel
like a burden
I've felt it a lot in my life – to family, friends, partner

I know if I told them, they'd have done whatever they
could to help me

But in that moment it seemed like the right thing to do
Pretty much everything is about, 'in that moment'

India Gibson

We need a new language

I think it is really important to note that when
somebody tries to end their life, inquests say:
     'Somebody successfully ended their life'.
What is successful about ending your life?
It conjures up the image of St Peter at the gate, with
'you came first' bags.

Obviously I'm going to get a badge when I get there at
some point, that says
'you failed to end your life'.

I think the language that's used around suicide is quite
damaging:

Someone *successfully* ends their life.
     Someone *failed* to take their life. Someone
     attempted and failed to take their life.
These narratives are very at odds with reality I feel.

I think a lot of the language around it needs to be
changed.

Someone contemplates taking their own life and gets
really close to it, and they get patched up and packed
off.

That doesn't work.
Because that doesn't change stuff.

I think what it clearly shows is,
that person is struggling.

And the things they don't need are: judgment, being labeled...
>   They don't need to be told they're bad;
>   They don't need to be burdened with family or
>   religious guilt.
What they do need is to be able to talk freely. About what they felt,
>   Why they felt it,
>   What made them feel it.

And each individual is different,
each experience is different.
>   One size will not fit all.

So there needs to be a clear way people then work together,
and also how the person can be helped to receive this.

How they can feel that they're worthy of it too.
That's a big part.

Elizabeth

THERE ARE
DIFFERENT
COLLORED
DRESSING
GOWNS

I am still here, I am still fighting. Every day is a battle against the world and myself but every day I get up and fight through. I know I can do it, I know I am strong enough to make it through. I am still here because I was and am strong enough. Every day I fight demons but they are in my head. I am real and the demons are not as strong as me!!!

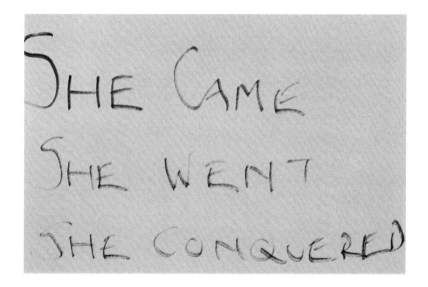

SHE CAME
SHE WENT
SHE CONQUERED

Having meaning is really essential.
There's 3 types of meaning:
> Positive,
> neutral
> and negative.

If you've neutral meaning or no meaning in your life,
then suicide becomes more of a risk.
Especially if you've got negative meaning.

But for a lot of people, they've got circumstances a bit
out of perspective, feeling they're a burden, or the
world would be better off without them,
or that they'd done something awful, which they
hadn't.

I don't want to eliminate the biochemical causes of
suicide. It could just be someone's lacking a certain
protein in their brain.

In my experience, more often than not, it's
distorted perspectives of circumstances
- that's 3 words together.

Those I think are the causes.
And lack of meaning is the main one:
Lack of meaning
and negative meaning.

I'm just drilling down into what we should be focused on,
which is the causes of depression and the turning points.

Andrew Welcome

New found hope

There was a voice a few months ago that said,
"You've pretty much defeated this"
 It was a positive voice.
"You've come out the other end."
To which I said,
"I hope so" and smiled.

I was in the house.
At first, I thought it was my mum.
Sounded like a female voice in her 40s or 50s.
I looked and checked -
There was no one there.

That's when I knew -
it was a positive hallucination.

Until then the voices I heard were disturbed and dark.
It felt good...
For once the voices were on my side.
Reflection:

It feels touching.
Good.
Positive.

Sam

KEEPS ME GOING

The only way I can describe it is – there's a little thing
in here, and it's so little, it's like a little voice
but it's getting louder.

It's just sort of, oh I don't know,
screaming out "No No,
why should I make it easy for them?"

The voice is getting louder,
now, it's "Do you know what?"
And I can feel it in my face type of thing
In my eyes, it's just like –
"Bollocks, I ain't fucking going off! Why should I?"

Think – I've come all this far
through so many battles
just to go 'Alright, I'll just crawl off and go and die
somewhere in a corner, quietly. Hey?'
That's why I would never do it you know in a barbaric
thing jumping in front of a car, anything like that.
That's what's been in my head
And I feel it, inside.

TJ Frost

Beyond recognition

I

My whole life is completely different.
Everything -
Everything is completely different.
My job, my ability to sit still.
Before I did the big suicide attempt, they diagnosed me
with Schizophrenia but I wasn't in any shape or form.
I was a very traumatised child.
Having worked through all that stuff, my life is beyond
recognition.
I am beyond recognition.
Incredibly, out of everybody I know, I am the happiest
person I know.
My glass is always half full -
It's usually full.
I am happy with myself.
Happy on the inside.

II

I didn't know what happiness was.
I knew what hedonism was, and I kind of knew how to
pretend to be happy, in a way, for some times.
I used to think, "Who are these people who are happy?
What do they do? How? Why? Contentment? What's
that?"

There were massive holes in me –

Massive spaces.

Totally empty on the inside.
I had incredibly low self-worth and low self-esteem -
Absolutely on the floor.
I have filled that spiritual void:
Spiritual connection to the universe -
To the self.

Sally Ann Cranage

Because I don't normally tell people how I feel
The main detail, not the gritty stuff
Just the "Oh, I miss Toby. I'm feeling down"
Not the stuff that's
Hiding
Behind it

Remember that I got through it before
I can do it again

India Gibson

WARRIOR

1.
That word – Warrior – it so resonates with me
oh God, yeah. I'm a bloody Warrior
Because it's like I have got this suit of armour on

It's funny – I don't look at that suit of armour as
protecting me
I think of that suit of armour as protecting them
Keeping the bad bits of me away from them, so I can
still help
It's like "What do you need? I'll get it for you"
"Don't you worry about that – I'll help you"
"What's that? You're hurting? About what?"
"Let's have a look what you need. We can do this."
It is always that thing – WE can do this

2.
It's silver, it's really thick and it's shiny.
It's pretty for other people to see.
It's not gonna hurt you. I'm not gonna hurt you.
It's that pretty wall.

It's not a horrible thing,
It's like "Come on — I can help you, I know I can help you".
It feels strong. Like a little cocoon around me.
No-one's gonna come in to get the ugly bit.
It's protected against the ugly but but I'm also okay.

It's giving me the strength to go "Okay then…"
It's giving me the strength from the inside – Out
And it is just that energy – that strong 'can do' energy
And it is going to be okay. It's gonna be okay

TJ Frost

Bottler

Round that time I got this tattoo
I used to be a bottler
So I got this bottle with flowers –
to represent talking about things
Being more open
And fluid
About things

Ethan Sheppard

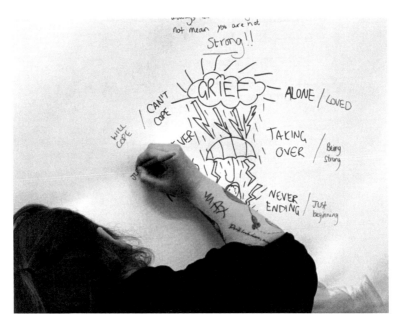

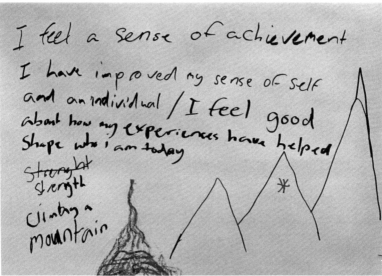

49

bobbing, surfing the waves, not afraid of sinking
buoyant

On paper

I think it's something that's always going to be in my
head.
But down on paper it's more truthful.
>   My feelings.

How much more I've understood about my suicidal
thoughts, than I ever thought I would.
>   My God.

Kat

Working on this project

Well, it's crystallised some of my thinking.
I've said a few things I wouldn't expect of myself, like
the jokes.
I suppose it's made me realise how far I've come.
        I've come a long way since then.

Yeah, I've come a long way from those dark times.
My days are filled with light.
And love.

And now people are coming to me, asking for my
opinions and advice.

Andrew Welcome

Or sometimes I feel like a tree.
When you asked, I was sitting there thinking 'How do I feel?'
That's why I drew the tree. Just like the tree – it was growing.

Other times I feel withered. Or like my leaves have been burnt.
It's not painful, but it's like they've been burnt.
Like I'm a withering little stick thing.
I just want to go 'It's ok, it will grow back'.

I wanted to put in big words CAN YOU SEE ME?

TJ Frost

Longing for the sea

She becomes human.
All selkies leave their skins,
They come off,
To become human,
Then, they put their skins back on -
and become seals

Someone has stolen her coat:
She has to walk in the world,
but it's really painful

I had this personal mythology -
(I don't think I have it anymore)
I am the selkie.
I can't bear the world,

but I can't find my coat -
Someone has stolen it.

A friend brought clothes her mother had thrown out.
There was this long black cardigan:
It was hideous.
I wore it to keep warm in the basement flat

One day another friend
Who knew my selkie secret
Saw me in it and said,
"You found your coat!"   *Lubna Gem Arielle*

It just makes me want to do everything for him

He was a right little hero when he was alive
He is my hero even more now

I just think of Toby as much as I can

My life is trying to keep his memory alive
Making sure he is never forgotten
That in itself gives me a purpose

India Gibson

It's nice to hear back

I had one drawing where it was me as a skull and a head
but outside of my head was a tornado –
and that is so prevalent to anyone, anyone who has
contemplated suicide or having depression
you are thinking all the time about something and
feeling numb at the same time
It's the most bizarre concept and behaviour
It's like you have no energy
You are always alone but you are always with your
thoughts and there is not a thing that just switches off
I feel like now the skull has filled in from my face and
there is no blood anymore
More picturesque but the tornado is still there.
And I think it's for everyone – the tornado is always
there. We've always got something to stress about
Always got something going on that we don't really
understand
We are worrying
But everyone has this thing

It's not letting that affect everything else.

So I feel I am not numb anymore.
I am accepting things about myself.
I am challenging myself – the way I think and the way I
behave.
And why I do that and just constantly progressing and
wanting to grow a bit more.
Trying to grow.   *Ethan Sheppard*

The Future

Oh God, it just – trying to sum it up…

It is big – and for the grabbing
The only way I can sum it up
What's coming to me now is…
Oh, it's so big

And
Flowers
I want to pick them, not to kill them
But because it is there for the taking
I want to pick the flowers –
Cos it's so beautiful
And I want to share the beauty.

There is things there for the
Taking – I can feel it – Opportunities

Here it comes, now –
Another door has opened.
That's what it feels like
Wow, that big heavy iron door has shut
And the pretty wooden one with grains of wood, black
knockers and all that (a round thing you turn with a nice
big latch on)
And I've gone like that
And it's 'Yes mate! I am through there!'
I'm going that way

Sod that - that way!

I lost my path, jumped off the path, went off
I don't know if it was overgrown or sort of withered
It was just – there was no path there
I think that's why I panicked and I was lost
– I was scared mate
I didn't know which way to turn,
I can see that now – there was no going passed
'Where do I go?' 'Where do I go?'

And all of a sudden there is a forest
A big door
And I can see the wood for the trees
Yeah. It's just mad!

TJ Frost

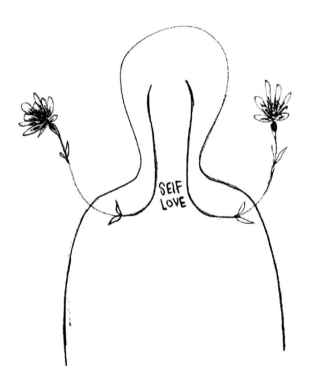

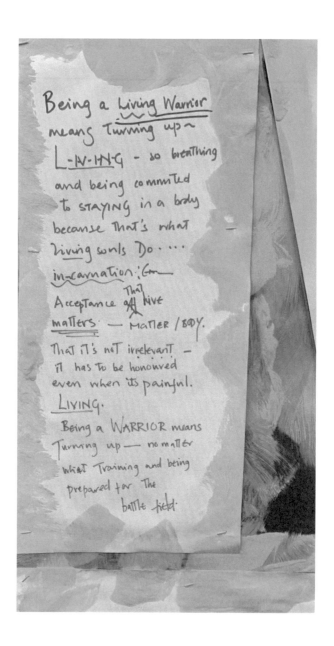

Being a Living Warrior
means Turning up~
L-IV-IN-G - so breathing
and being committed
to STAYING in a body
because That's what
living souls Do····
incarnation: ~~~~
Acceptance of <ins>That</ins> live
matters - MATTER / BODY.
That it's not irrelevant -
it has to be honoured
even when its painful.
LIVING.
Being a WARRIOR means
Turning up — no matter
what Training and being
prepared for The
battle field.

60

Thank you to everyone involved in the Living Warrior project. Including: All the staff at Folkestone Library; Diane Dever; Greg Taylor; Finding Eanswyth project; Hollie Brennan; Jack Mitcham; Jonathan Pratt; KCC; Lauretta Kavanagh; Lynsey Illet; Mitchell Bloomfield; NHS Kent and Medway. Most importantly thanks to all the warriors – rage on. Protect and push: Thanks to - our guardian of the warriors and expert cow bell ringer Madlin Brinton; Living Words Warrior writers – Anil Sebastian, Shazea Qurasihi and Susanna Howard; and our ultimate Living Warriors – Andrew Welcome; Elizabeth; Ethan Sheppard; India Gibson; Lubna Gem Arielle; Kat; Sally Ann Cranage; Sam; & TJ Frost.

This project is part of the Saving Lives Suicide Prevention Innovation Fund. Funded by KCC.

CONTACT
Living Words
www.livingwords.org.uk
info@livingwords.org.uk
07967502506
Facebook: /livingwords.org.uk
Twitter: @LivingWordsUK
Insta: LivingWordsUK
c/o GF01, The Glassworks
Mill Bay, Folkestone CT20 1JR

charity #: 1157780

If you need help, please reach out and speak to someone. If you would prefer to speak to someone you don't know, these helplines are all available 24 hours a day:

Release The Pressure
In Kent, we have a highly trained and experienced team available 24/7 to provide you with confidential support to get you back on track.
Freephone: 0800 107 0160

Mental Health Matters
Freephone: 0800 107 0160

Samaritans
Freephone: 116 123

LIVING WORDS
Keep Talking. You matter.
Keep Listening. It matters how we listen.

"It's not 'Hey, hey look at me' It's 'Hey. LISTEN to me."
TJ Frost